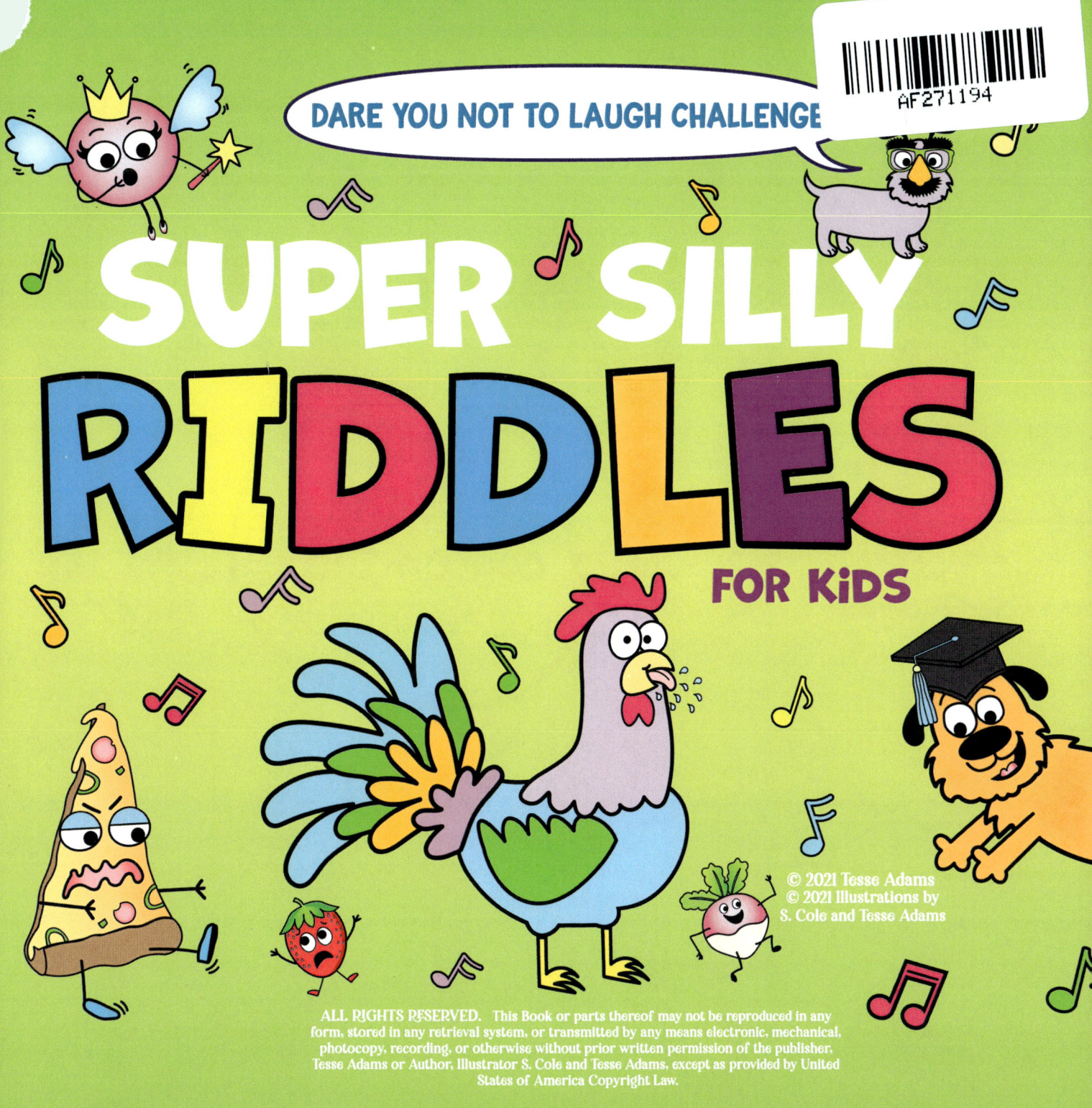

DARE YOU NOT TO LAUGH CHALLENGE

SUPER SILLY
RIDDLES
FOR KIDS

© 2021 Tesse Adams
© 2021 Illustrations by
S. Cole and Tesse Adams

LOOK!
There is someone here who wants to play the DARE YOU NOT to Laugh Challenge!

The rules are simple, you cannot laugh when you read this book.

In fact, we DOUBLE DOG DARE YOU NOT to laugh, giggle, grin, roll your eyes OR smile when you read this book!

Not even ONE little, teeny-weeny, itsy-bitsy smile.

Ahem.

Good Luck.

Why were the pillows mad at each other?

Because they were having a PILLOW FIGHT!

What follows a unicorn wherever she goes?

Her tail!

What kind of spider spends a lot of time at the gym?

Daddy STRONG legs!

What time is it when you see 100 angry bees?

Time to run!

What kind of food has a lot of money?

A fortune cookie!

What makes more noise than a dinosaur?

Two dinosaurs!

Why do hummingbirds hum?

Because they don't know the words!

What kind of toys do centipedes play with?

iSO-9ET

How do monkeys get down the stairs fast?

They slide down the BANANA-ster!

What kind of balls do not bounce?

snowballs!

What kind of cup cannot hold water?

A cupcake!

What side of a pig has the most mud?

The outside!

I am scary, but I am very sweet. What am I?

Halloween!

What do ducks like in their tacos?

QUACK-amole!

What did the big firecracker say to the little firecracker?

My Pop is bigger than your Pop!

What do you call a fairy that does not take a bath?

Stinkerbell!

What gets wet as it dries?

A towel!

When do cows like to sing?

When they are in the MOOO-d!

What color eggs do roosters lay?

None, because roosters don't lay eggs!

What has four legs and flies?

A picnic table!

What lives if it eats but dies if it drinks?

Fire!

What is the most unhappy fruit?

A crab apple!

What kind of dolls do pirates play with?

B-AAARRR-bie!

What is brown and sticky?

A stick!

What kind of music do you find in a refrigerator?

Cool music!

What stinks and goes up and down?

A skunk in an elevator!

What has two legs, but cannot walk?

A pair of pants!

Why was the basketball player wearing a bib?

Because he was dribbling everywhere!

How do you make a cream puff?

Make him run around the block a few times!

A fris-bee!

Books by Tesse Adams

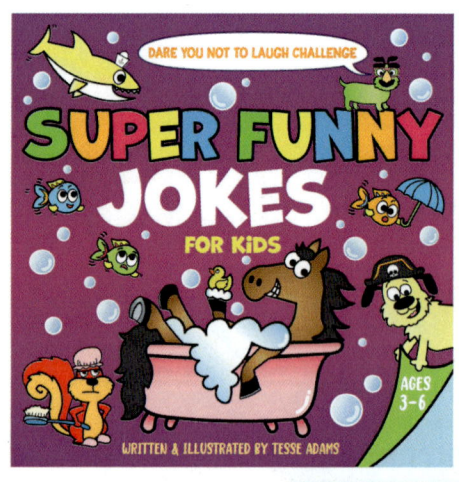

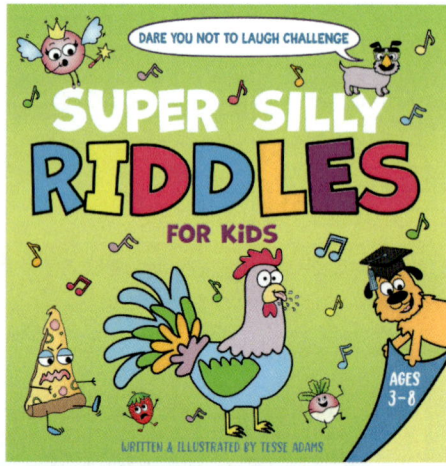

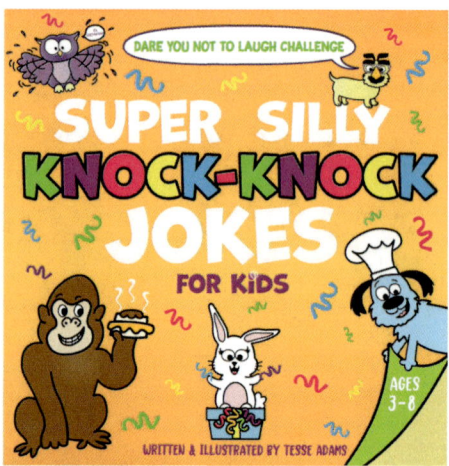

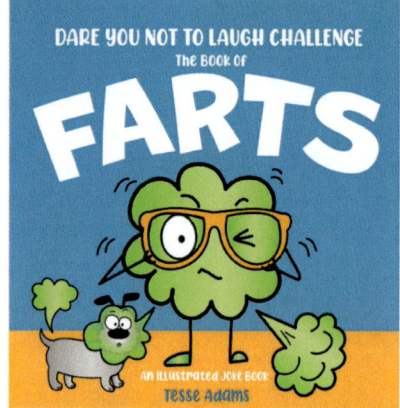

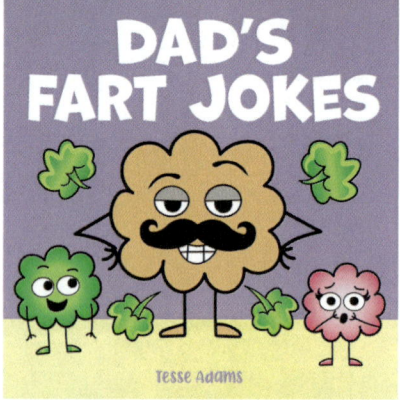

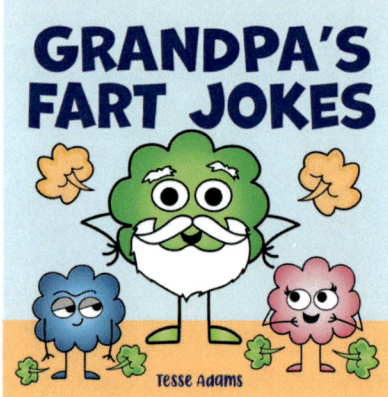

Made in the USA
Coppell, TX
01 April 2023

15040925R00026